Engaged for Growth!

Rules of Engagement and Leadership Secrets

Engaging Employees, Increasing Productivity

and Growing your Bottom Line!

Renée Cormier

Manor House

Library and Archives Canada
Cataloguing in Publication

Cormier, Renée, 1963-
Engaged for growth! : the rules of engagement and leadership
secrets for engaging employees, increasing productivity and
growing your bottom line!
/ Renée Cormier.

ISBN 978-1-897453-28-5

1. Leadership. 2. Management. 3. Employees--Attitudes.
4. Employee morale. I. Title.

HD57.7.C67 2009   658.3'14
C2010-900317-9

First Edition.
96 pages.
All rights reserved.

Cover design: Michael B. Davie and Donovan Davie
Published December 15, 2009
Manor House Publishing Inc.
www.manor-house.biz
(905) 648-2193

Manor House gratefully acknowledges the financial support of
the Government of Canada through the Book Publishing Industry
Development Program (BPIDP), Dept. of Canadian Heritage, for
our publishing activities.

For more information contact:
Renée Cormier, Employee Engagement Specialist
POWERHOUSE CONFERENCES 905-593-2778
Blog: http://reneecormier.wordpress.com
Website: www.powerconferences.ca or www.reneecormier.com.

Foreword

I wrote this book because I am passionate about working with business leaders to create work environments that drive positive business results.

Given the statistics and the state of the economy, I feel there is a strong need for businesses to work toward changing their corporate culture.

According to extensive studies by Gallup Management Journal, disengaged employees cost US businesses over $300 billion annually. Gallup also determined the sole cause of disengagement among employees is bad managers. Leaders, who don't lead effectively and don't know how to gain willing cooperation from others, create disastrous results and actually harm the economy.

According to the GMJ study, only 29% of employees are engaged in their work, so for every million dollars a company puts out in payroll, they are only receiving $290,000 worth of effort. That means that $710,000 of payroll is being wasted on employees who are apathetic and causing customers to run to the competition.

There are two reasons that I decided to become a self-employed training professional who specializes in Employee Engagement: First, the thought of working for someone else terrifies me. I've had my share of bad bosses over the years, and to be fair, I've had some pretty good ones, too. The bad bosses, however, really left a mark on me. Let me clarify: The *abusive* bosses left a mark on me.

The others simply left me with a negative impression, which is the second reason I decided to do what I do for a living. The teacher in me wants to show leaders how to get the most out of their employees and the idealist in me envisions being able to work with others to create healthy and productive work environments everywhere.

I get enormous satisfaction from providing meaningful guidance to leaders at all levels of an organization and from watching them create powerful teams that get things done and contribute to the bottom line.

It absolutely thrills me to hear my clients tell me I made a difference in the way they work with their employees and that the results of the changes they made are very favourable. That's how I know I am doing the right thing. I was meant to be self-employed and I was meant to show others how to not be complacent and settle for mediocrity.

It is in that spirit that I write this book. I fully intend to create a book that is genuinely helpful to those who read it, and it is my sincere hope that those who need it the most will find it on their desks and take my instruction to heart. That's the idealist speaking.

The realist in me knows that people who strive for continuous self-improvement will devour this book and that those who look for inspiration will likely find what they're looking for. Likewise, those who read to be reminded of what they already know will appreciate this book's content. I am grateful for you for reading this book and hope you'll recommend it to any business that wants to grow.
- **Renée Cormier**

Acknowledgements

Writing a book is a real accomplishment. It's not entirely an easy thing to do, but I think I have been blessed with a gift for writing, which makes it easier for me more than others. I always knew I had at least one book in me. I have to thank my mother for always encouraging me to write one. She had fiction in mind, but I think I'm more of a non-fiction kind of gal.

Business books really light my fire, and being able to write about what inspires me gives me enormous pleasure. I should thank my brother David for turning me on to the books that changed my life so many years ago.

Thanks should also go to my friend Skip Green who encouraged me to read **The Dip**, by Seth Godin. That book pushed me to do what I never seemed to get around to doing, and I guess I should thank Seth for inspiring me.

Special thanks to my husband, Marty, for patiently putting up with me, providing valuable input and being such a good friend and lover.

Thanks also to friend and fashion consultant, Kelly Golby of Dezire Boutique in Whitby, Ontario, for providing me with such a terrific outfit for my cover. Tu es très chic!

Michael Davie, I must thank you for allowing me this opportunity. I appreciate your help, making it easy for me to complete this book. Thanks also to Mary Ellen for telling me about Michael and Manor House Publishing.

Chapter 1

"Avoid having your ego so close to your position that when your position falls, your ego goes with it."
– Colin Powell

The only thing worse than being a bad leader, is being a bad leader with no desire to be better.

I always say that ego is the greatest enemy of leadership because it is your ego that will interfere with your ability to improve. Your ego tells you, "I don't need to be better" but the ego gives you a road you can run down endlessly and takes you far from the truth. Ego-dominated managers are actually cowards, who are filled with fear and who are unwilling to face the truth about themselves.

Ego is a defence mechanism and as a defence mechanism, ego overcompensates for feelings of ineptitude by trying to keep others from looking good. Ego-dominated bosses therefore, tend to do things like withhold information, devalue employees, compete with employees, dismiss input from employees, etc. The list of behaviours could go on forever, but the source is always the same: fear.

Deep down, ego-dominated managers fear people will see them as the inept creatures they really are. They are misguided in believing that as the boss, they are supposed to have all the answers. The truth is, the best leaders intentionally surround themselves with the most capable and talented people and the worst leaders intentionally surround themselves with the most incompetent people. Both leaders want to look good, but the ego-dominated manager/leader sees star employees as potential threats, so he seeks out all the yes-men and lackeys he can find. They make him feel strong and important. They constantly suck up to him and feed his ego. Employees showing creativity, strong capability and intelligence aren't appreciated by an ego-dominated manager/leader, and they may well find themselves constructively dismissed if they don't quit first.

I think it is fair to say that most of us have seen our share of ego-dominated managers. It is important to know that even good leaders can fall into ego traps from time to time. We are all human after all. Great leadership requires a person to be able to recognize when the ego is rising to the forefront and controlling our behaviour. As a leader, it is also a requirement to keep your ego in check.

In the name of continuous improvement, sales people are often instructed to do a parking lot analysis after a sales call to see what they could have done better. It is a strategy that leaders can use as well. It is well worth your while to take the time to review each day's events and see whether or not there was something that should have been handled differently.

Reflection is important if you want to grow as a leader. You cannot change what you don't acknowledge, so taking the time to reflect on your day will allow you to face yourself and address problems that need to be worked out.

Common Ego-Dominated Behaviours:

- Withholding information

- Devaluing employees

- Competitiveness/ looking out for yourself only

- Being dismissive

- Always having to be right/ wanting to have all the answers

- Not taking responsibility for the errors of the team

- Feeling you are smarter or better than the team

- Being manipulative

- Taking credit for achievements you didn't earn

- Failing to give credit to those deserving it

- Power tripping

Effective management is vital to all organizations. The term "effective management" is actually grossly inadequate. Most people speak of leadership nowadays because "managers" are seen as either paper shufflers or people who walk around and intimidate employees. Leaders, on the other hand, empower people to get things done. They inspire greatness in others and they generate results that far outweigh the results of their "manager" co-workers.

Gallup Management Journal regularly conducts and publishes the results of their studies of Employee Engagement. These studies are the result a highly refined set of questions given to employees in a cross section of companies of all sizes and industries in both unionized and non-unionized environments and the results only ever vary slightly from year to year.

What you need to know: According to these surveys, only 29% of employees are actually engaged at work. The top 29% carry the bulk of the work, they generate the most revenue and they love their jobs! But 54% of employees are disengaged. For them, work is a means to pay the bills. It's just a job. They are never inspired, they will call in sick if they wake up with a slight headache, they leave early, if they can and they don't care what happens to the company or its customers. The remaining 17% are considered to be actively disengaged. We've all worked with them. Some of us have even become them. Some of them have seen a lot of changes and have a long history with the company. They are jaded because they have been repeatedly disappointed. They are angry and have become saboteurs. They want everyone to be on their side and they spend an enormous amount of time trying to convert people. This group has a complete lack of respect for the leadership of the company. They are really bad news.

Gallup also reports that disengaged employees cost U.S. companies over 3 billion dollars annually! If you're wondering where that figure comes from, consider the cost of turnover, sick days, stress leave, lost customers due to poor customer service, workplace injuries, consumer health where your company's product is tainted as a result of workplace apathy, and the list goes on. Disengaged employees cause a company to slide down a slippery rope.

Do you know what the sole cause of employee disengagement is? Once again, according to Gallup Management Journal, it is **bad managers.** Your employees will make you or break you. That's why it is well worth your while to invest in improving your leadership skills and work on creating an engaged culture.

It is management that directly affects the culture of a company and since management is always concerned about bottom line results, it behoves them to strive to be the best leaders they can be. According to Gallup, disengaged employees don't recommend their employers' products or services to people and they don't recommend their company as an employment source.

Why is this important? Ok, the first one's a no-brainer. If you don't recommend products or services, then nobody buys. The second one is also important because your talent pool will become very shallow if your company has a reputation for being terrible to work for. I personally have heard it about lots of companies. In fact, my family doctor once commented that she had heard my employer at the time was terrible to work for. She heard right.

The Internet is also a great way of spreading the word about which companies are terrible to work for, and people use it. Just check out the comments on Forbes magazine's list of top 100 companies. Tons of people comment on their employers, both past and present, and a lot of it is quite unfavourable! If your company is seen in that light, then you will never be able to attract the brightest and the best employees. There's some food for thought if you are finding your list of job candidates to be low calibre.

How does ego figure into all of this? It's simple. Bosses with big egos negatively affect employee engagement. Who wants to work for an egomaniac? Look back at your past bosses or even at your current one, if you have one. Can you recall any instances where his ego got in the way of productivity? Do you remember your reaction or the reaction of your co-workers? Do you think your ego gets in the way of engaging your people? What could you do differently?

I have composed what I call The Ten Commandments of Leadership. It is intentionally written in a mix of archaic and modern language, as opposed to the strictly archaic biblical form most people would expect. Initially, when I first wrote this, it was written in the negative, similarly to the way it is written in the Bible. A couple of people smartly pointed out to me the benefits of writing it in the positive, so I rewrote it and will present it to you in this book. Before I do that, though, I would like you in all sincerity to use it as part of your daily assessment.

Ask yourself whether or not you have broken any of those commandments and what you can do to (A) repair the damage and (B) take action to produce the results you want. Please remember that you cannot change what you don't acknowledge, so be painfully honest with yourself. In the the Leadership Development section of this book you will find self-reflection exercises that will help you.

Renée's Ten Commandments of Leadership:

Commandment #1

Thou must guide, mentor and coach your people.

Your employees are your greatest competitive advantage, not your products or your services. They need you to support them, not tell them what to do. They need to benefit from your experience and they need to trust that you will back them if things go sideways.

Independent thinking should be encouraged, not discouraged – provided the intentions are good, of course.

Commandment #2

Thou must set a fine personal example for integrity and professionalism.

You cannot engage your employees if you have questionable character. A boss who is having an affair, who is known to steal, lie or undermine others is not a leader.

Such a person could never command the respect of others, and without that he cannot effectively lead. Certainly you will not engage your employees if you are of questionable character.

Leaders should be trustworthy and very transparent so that their integrity never gets questioned.

Commandment # 3

Thou must provide positive feedback.

It's unfortunate that leaders often forget to tell their people what they are doing right but always remember to tell them what they are doing wrong. Dale Carnegie once said, "There is no such thing as constructive criticism."
Criticism deflates, de-motivates and destroys confidence no matter how you try to "sandwich" it. Its very nature is destructive. If you can establish a non-threatening relationship with your employees, they should have no trouble telling you what went wrong and what they could do differently next time. Providing continuous positive feedback is one way to develop trust and build rapport.

Commandment #4

Thou must always make decisions.

Making no decision is worse than making the wrong decision. An unwillingness to take chances is also an unwillingness to learn.

When you don't make decisions, you stand in the way of growth and you continually frustrate your team.

As a leader, you don't need to make all of the decisions, but when it's time to haul sail, you had better decide to move! Things need to move forward and decisions need to be made to get you there. Action requires a concise decision, which brings us to the next commandment.

Commandment #5

Thou must take action.

As Larry the Cable Guy says, "Git 'er done!" Don't stand in the way of growth by doing nothing. Indecision and inaction will cause your team to lose faith in your ability to lead and could spark mutiny. Disgruntled employees will work against you every step of the way, and if the opportunity arises, they'll see you get fired. If you're not sure what to do, ask for input from your team. That is what they're there for. They're your support, and you are theirs.

Commandment #6

Thou must give clear direction.

Don't expect people to just know what you want. If you have a specific outcome that must be achieved in a certain way and by a particular time, then you had better be very clear about your expectations.

Employees who don't know what is expected of them at work become disengaged. They float around like little lost souls, wasting their time on all sorts of things because they have no clear idea of the expectations. They bring you a completed project and you are unhappy because it wasn't done right, or was incomplete. You blame the employee for being incompetent, but you really must blame yourself.

If you were clear about your expectations and provided feedback at appropriate times, you wouldn't be upset about the outcome. Lack of clear direction impedes progress. Most leaders have expectations, but those expectations will never be met if they are not clearly articulated.

Commandment #7

Thou must empower your people.

If you empower your people, you won't have to baby-sit all day! I can't tell you how many managers have complained to me that they feel like overpaid babysitters, or that they can't get anything done because they spend the entire day putting out fires. If that's what your work life is like, then your people are not empowered.

The trouble is that many leaders really don't know how to empower their people. Empowerment is a big subject, so I'll address that in more detail later on.

Commandment #8

Thou must accept responsibility for the shortcomings of your team.

Don't go beating up on your employees when things go awry. Take it personally, because it is personal. You, as leader, are responsible for all outcomes. If they goof up, it is because you didn't communicate effectively.

If you communicate clearly, establish trust, provide continual feedback and properly empower your team, your results will be phenomenal. Anything short of that is because you, the leader, slipped up.

Put your ego aside and you will see what you did wrong. Then allow yourself to grow.

Commandment #9

Thou must accept input from your team.

No one can be successful without the support of others. That's important, so I will repeat it. No one can be successful without the support of others. As a leader, you don't need to have all the answers. You just need to know how to get the most out of people so that as a unit you can come up with all the answers. The more heads on a problem the better. The folks on the ground will often know a lot more than their manager about what is really going on with the business. Take advantage of that fact and allow them to help you progress.

Commandment #10

Thou must establish trust.

Establishing trust means doing what you say you will do, being 100% dependable, being completely honest, taking a genuine interest in people, and demonstrating a high degree of integrity every single day. By failing to establish trust you jeopardize the success of the team. When your employees don't trust you, they will work behind your back to sabotage the business. That's employee disengagement at its worst.

Leaders who live by the 10 commandments I've just outlined must be willing to let go of their ego. The higher up you are in an organization, the more difficult that becomes, but it is imperative if you are going to create a culture that is conducive to employee engagement. Ego-dominated managers will never be able to engage their employees, nor will they be able to command respect, empower their employees, motivate their employees, or generate the kind of bottom line results that non ego dominated managers generate.

Culture is created from the top on down, not the middle on down. A leader can control the outcomes of his or her team but cannot control the overall culture of an organization unless the leader is at the top. Top level leaders who work toward creating an engaged culture ensure that all leaders in the organization are working toward building a high level of employee engagement.

Prominent online retailer Zappos CEO Tony Hsieh (pron. Shay) has developed huge success by keeping the workplace a light-hearted environment. From his cubicle (yes, his cubicle) he focuses on developing a strong and healthy culture at Zappos and with over $1 billion in revenue in 2008, business leaders could learn a lot from Tony Hsieh. Tony understands that a healthy corporate culture translates into phenomenal customer experiences and repeat business (75% of their customer orders on any given day are from repeat customers).

Prior to heading up Zappos, Tony co-founded LinkExchange, which he later sold to Microsoft because he didn't like the culture. Perhaps at the time Tony understood the importance of having a strong corporate culture, but didn't quite know how to create one. It would appear he has learned a few things since then.

The rewards of creating an engaged culture are significant. Most companies don't publish the results of their engagement surveys, but Campbell Soup Company does. That's likely because Campbell's has something to be proud of, whereas most other companies do not.

Campbell's was recognized by Gallup as one of the best places to work in America in both 2007 and 2008.

According to the statistics published on Campbell's website, their employee engagement scores have risen dramatically since 2001 when Campbell's reported a 2:1 ratio between engaged and disengaged employees. Most companies, by the way, have a ratio of 1:3.

In 2008 the level of engagement at Campbell's rose to 12:1 making their overall score 79%. – that's 50% higher than the American average. That means that for every million dollars Campbell's spends on payroll, they get $790,000 worth of productivity whereas other companies only get $290,000 worth. To make that even clearer, the average company loses $710,000 for every million it spends on payroll. Campbell's, on the other hand, is losing $210,000 for every million.

That gives Campbell's a huge competitive advantage, but it's still too much money to lose. That is why Campbell's is working toward improving their results yearly. This is a prime example of how the top of an organization can impact the overall culture and produce bottom line results. You can now get full details of Campbell's report at: http://www.campbellsoupcompany.com/csr/workplace_eng agement.asp.

Chapter 2

"Character is the firm foundation stone upon which one must build to win respect. Just as no worthy building can be erected on a weak foundation, so no lasting reputation worthy of respect can be built on a weak character."
- R. C. Samsel

It seems you can't talk about the **Ten Commandments of Leadership** without also discussing the **Seven Virtues of Leadership**, so this chapter is dedicated to the virtues. All of these character traits are important in your quest to develop an engaged culture. If people are going to respect you, they will respect you for who you really are.

Since your actions are a reflection of your character, it is important to examine your character during the process of developing your leadership skills. Leadership is probably more about who you are than it is about what you do, so look inside yourself and see where you need to focus your energy. We all have our inadequacies, but we make choices about the kind of person we want to be. Great leaders make great choices and they achieve great results because of those choices.

People trust virtuous leaders. Virtuous leaders are able to rally more support than non-virtuous leaders, and they produce better results and sustain growth better than their non-virtuous counterparts, no matter what the economic climate is. Former Polish President Lech Walesa, for example, not only changed a nation, but changed the world as we knew it in the 1980s and is still regarded as a trustworthy leader by Polish people today.

Virtuous leaders don't need to search for excuses for failure, because they are truly successful people. True success, by the way, can only be achieved through integrity. Engaging in criminal activity may make you rich, but it will not make you successful.

The Seven Virtues of Leadership

- Continuous Self-Improvement

- Dedication

- Sincerity

- Generosity

- Humility

- Integrity

- Wisdom

Virtue #1: Continuous Self-Improvement

Continuous self- improvement is the duty of every leader. We can never know it all and we need constant reminding of everything we do know. Continually searching for knowledge and striving to be better at what you do, will give you a professional edge and keep you feeling energized. Leaders can develop their skills by a building personal library of business books which deal with the subjects of leadership, communication, employee motivation, etc. (be sure to actually read your books).

You can also learn things from co-workers and team members, not just about leadership, but about everything that relates to your work.

The best way to improve your skills is to continually assess them. As I mentioned previously, reflecting on your actions and determining what you could have done better is very important in your development as a leader who engages employees.

Of course all of that means nothing if you are not committed to making changes, so please make sure you are committed to being better. Getting the results you really want requires commitment.

Virtue # 2: Dedication

Dedication and dependability are at the core of every great leader. Be committed to fulfilling promises and completing tasks on time. Doing what you say you are going to do will gain you a lot of respect from others.

Whenever you take on a task, keep the end result in mind. It is important to continually remind yourself of your purpose and to strive to achieve the best results.

Remain focused on your goals and don't allow yourself to be distracted by pettiness. Sometimes that's easier said than done, but it is what successful leaders do.

Virtue # 3: Sincerity

People respect sincerity in others. If you speak the truth and speak from your heart, people will always trust you. If you say only what people want to hear, or if you endeavour to flatter those around you, then your attempts to charm will fall flat at least half the time.

When speaking to people, make sure you offer a sincere smile and make people feel genuinely important. That cannot be accomplished by uttering false statements. True leaders act in service of others and try to see other points of view. In doing so, they make others feel important. Valuing other people's feelings and opinions is an important element of Leadership.

Virtue #4: Generosity

Be generous with your time so that you can assist others whenever necessary. In his book, ***How to Win Friends and Influence People***, Dale Carnegie advises us to "be lavish in sincere praise." There is absolutely no reason to refrain from telling someone they did a great job or that they impress you in some way as long as you are being truthful.

When people present their ideas to you, be supportive rather than contrary. If you don't like the idea, gently explain your concern and make an effort to see the good in it. Do everything you possibly can to show that you appreciate others ideas and efforts. Great leaders do this on a daily basis.

Don't wait for performance reviews to give feedback to people. A little positive feedback every day will take you a very long way in your journey toward creating an engaged workforce.

Virtue #5: Humility

Ego is a lack of humility, but those with huge egos are easily humiliated. Your employees are your support and they will make you successful. Give credit to all who have helped you along the way, and allow others to shine. When they shine, you shine as well.

Allow others to suggest improvements and act on them. Decide that you do not always have to be right and that not all ideas need to be yours. Choose your battles carefully. Some people just want to fight and be the winner, whether they are right or not. That is their ego talking and that is a big no-no for leaders.

If you make a mistake, admit it right away. Next, apologize, and do whatever you need to do to make things right. Speak about your own mistakes and what you learned from them rather than pointing out the mistakes of others. This builds trust and gives people the opportunity to learn from you without feeling threatened.

Virtue #6: Integrity

Never do anything you need to be ashamed of. If you do something you wouldn't want your mother or your children to know, then that it a pretty good indication that you are acting without integrity.

If you think people won't find out about your conduct, then you are a fool who is only fooling herself. Somebody will catch you and they will blab about it, too. Act according to what is best for others rather than what is best for you and always be consistent in doing "the right thing."

Virtue #7: Wisdom

Wise people take the opportunity to learn from the mistakes of others as well as their own. It helps enormously in the decision-making process. Wise people also examine all possible outcomes prior to acting. They like to look at the big picture and consider the long-term effect of a decision.

Wise leaders don't put off making decisions. They act quickly, but not hastily. They arm themselves with facts, consider all points of view and remain objective. They do not get caught up in emotion or hype. This allows them to make prudent decisions.

Practicing the virtues means being the best you can be, all the time. Don't be fooled into thinking that your home life and work life can be different. You can't be virtuous at work and a sleazebag after 5:00 pm. In order to live the virtues effectively and see the benefits in your business, you need to be able to integrate them into your character.

If you want to know something about a person's character, check his values. I often do an exercise with my clients to see what their values are. I always find it interesting; especially when integrity and honesty don't even register.

I think it is a good practice to give a values assessment to people before you hire them. Culturally, it is good to know if your job candidate shares values that are compatible with your organizational values. You'd also want to know if your financial manager lacks integrity. It would be better to not have to find that out the hard way!

The decisions we make reflect our values and our integrity. Business leaders who lack integrity steal from people. Bernie Madoff gained the trust of a large number of people and their charitable organizations. No one questioned his integrity. No one really knew what he valued. They trusted him because they trusted his clients and his position as chairman of Nasdaq. His decisions and lack of integrity hurt a lot of people, and ultimately hurt him.

Who you know and what you own don't always reveal a lot about your character. Driving a nice car and hob knobbing with the rich and famous really doesn't say anything about what really matters. What matters most in leadership is the depth and quality of your character. Leaders who behave ethically and adhere to high moral standards are ultimately more successful than those who don't.

If you examine the times when things go wrong for well known leaders, you will notice that it is usually when they get caught doing something that is reprehensible. Bill Clinton was never as well thought of after fooling around with Monica Lewinski and Conrad Black is no longer revered as a great business leader since he has been convicted of fraud and obstruction of justice. Most people will never fully trust them.

What you do and how you treat people cause people to make judgements about your character and those judgements can harm your business for a long time afterward. I know of a company where the CEO had an affair with his assistant and even though the affair is long over, people still mention it. That stupid affair still has employees talking more than 20 years later and it still affects the credibility of the company's leadership. You must realize that anything that affects the leader's credibility will affect employee performance.

Leaders who drink at business events also put themselves at a huge disadvantage. If you have to have a drink to be sociable, be smart and limit it to one. After that, switch over to soft drinks. Alcohol has a way of making people say and do things they regret later. Having a clear head will lessen the likelihood that you will behave badly.

Failing to treat people with respect and dignity, swearing around the office, fudging numbers in reports to make your results look plumper; all of these things will cause people to question your integrity. As leader, it is essential that people trust you and think of you as someone with a high degree of professionalism and strong moral fibre.

If you think you can do illicit things and that no one will find out, think again. People always find out, and even if they only suspect you have been naughty, they will tell everyone who will listen. Once that happens, it will haunt you forever.

There is a lot to be said for self-restraint in leadership. Controlling your most base desires may not seem like a lot of fun, but leaders who are able to keep their emotions and appetites in check will find it easier to gain the respect of others. That respect will allow you to influence people's decisions, and build greater opportunities for your business.

Chapter 3

"The best executive is the one who has sense enough to pick good men to do what he wants done, and self-restraint enough to keep from meddling with them while they do it."
-Theodore Roosevelt

A VP of Human Resources once commented to me that many companies find it challenging to get their employees to use their best judgement in doing what is best for their customers. I recognize this challenge as being the by-product of fear-based leadership and an un-empowered workforce.

A lot of frontline employees are very reluctant to take initiative and use their "discretionary judgement" to help their customers because they simply don't have any real authority. They may be told they do, but often when they do use that special tool in their kit bag, they receive flak from their boss and are chided for being out of line.

There are a lot of problems, here. The first problem is the unskilled leader, and the second is the company culture that considers its frontline people to be imbeciles. The fact is that even in this day and age, there are many companies who discourage creative thinking in their employees. This is particularly true in the manufacturing industry, but in other areas as well.

Behavioural psychologists know that you get what you reward. This is true for humans and animals alike no matter where you are in the world. People respond to the reactions they get.

When the reaction is favourable, you will get more of that behaviour. When the reaction is unfavourable, you will get less of it. If you genuinely want to retain customers, then, you need to empower your people and reward them for their efforts. A kind word goes a long way, in this case.

As I mentioned in the first chapter, ego-dominated leaders are bad for business. If you want great business results, you have to let go of your ego.

Mission, Vision and Values

Many companies do not involve employees in the mission, vision and values of the company. In fact, there are many companies that haven't even articulated what they are. Not having clear mission/vision statements allows you to run the risk of creating a sort of organized chaos.

Without a clear vision, everyone will be running in different directions. If the left hand never seems to know what the right hand is doing, then you probably are not sharing the same mission and vision. You are also not communicating effectively. If everything you do in your company is a reflection of the mission, vision and values, you will get to where you need to be a lot faster.

The first step in creating an engaged culture is to make sure everyone understands and lives by the mission, vision and values of the company. It is also a part of empowerment, in my opinion, because your employees need to know what they are there for. They need to know how they contribute to the success of the company.

If you are going to let them provide input and make decisions, then it is imperative that they know exactly where you want to go and which values need to be considered when making those decisions.

Whenever I visit a company for the first time, I often ask the receptionist if she knows the mission, vision and values of the company. You would be surprised how many have said things like, "They sent it to us. I think I have it in an email somewhere." In one company I visited, there were three or four people scrambling to find it (and they couldn't). No one knew it.

Sadly, I even came across several companies where the front line staff didn't even know the name of the president. Can you imagine that? What kind of results do these CEOs expect to generate when the people at the face of their company don't even know what they are there for or who signs their cheques? Do you think they feel that their work is important to the success of the company? Not likely.

You have to think of your business like the inside of a watch. All parts work in unison to keep time. If a part of your watch is not working properly, then the best outcome is that your watch will be slow. The worst, of course, is that it will not work at all. Having a slow watch, however, means that you will miss opportunities you could have otherwise had. Don't be content to put up with a slow watch. It's costing you money.

Living the company values is as important as understanding the mission and vision.

It's interesting to see how some companies present a list of values to their employees. Out of nowhere people are told, "Hang these in your offices and in the corridors. These are our values." No one ever asked the employees to contribute to the list, and no one ever spoke of them outside of a closed boardroom, and suddenly they appear. Everyone reads the values and rolls their eyes in disgust because none of the upper managers had ever lived by them and everyone doubted that they would change just because they are written down for all to see.

I know of one company where the values were literally ripped off the walls leaving clearly visible holes (now *there's* a cry for help). I once worked with a client who told me not to talk about their company's values with the managers because it was a sore spot and could stir up a lot of trouble. That's a shame. Think of Commandment # 2 (Set a fine example of integrity and professionalism).

Live the values. Before you make decisions, check to make sure they are consistent with the values.

Revise your values from time to time and make sure your employees provide input. Have each work group develop an additional set of values to reflect what they want for their team. For example, co-operation with other employees may not be on the company's values list, but is probably one of those unwritten rules. Until your team writes it down, though, it is not official. Having it agreed upon and written down gives you the opportunity to more effectively meet deadlines.

If a team mate is not living the value, then you can call her on it and correct the problem immediately. No one will have to walk around frustrated because Mary is being difficult.

EllisDon Corporation has developed a thriving corporate culture based on living the company values alone. They don't bother with mission statements, believing the journey is more important. The company is consistently listed on Canada's Top 50 Employers list, and if you browse through their website, you will quickly see why.

CEO Geoff Smith understands that his people are his greatest competitive advantage and has a set of company values that would be especially appealing to innovative, action-oriented people.

These values create a fertile environment for employees to become truly empowered. They are trust, entrepreneurial enthusiasm, individual initiative, complete openness and mutual accountability.

I have to say, I admire EllisDon's commitment to its values, as well as the value they place on their employees. If everyone made their employees the focus of their business, and not their shareholders, they would reap the same benefits. I'm excited to see that Geoff Smith gets it!

Empowerment

Empowered employees are engaged employees. You can't have one without the other, but do you know what a truly empowered employee looks like? Employee Empowerment is not a well understood term. Many leaders have no real idea how to empower their people. They just know that it is something that is supposed to be good for the work environment. Because they don't really understand how to create an empowered team, they often make mistakes that have disastrous consequences.

Empowerment isn't about letting your employees run amuck. It is about giving people the tools and the trust they need to make decisions that are helpful to the business. It is also about allowing them to use their creativity to find answers and take your business to new heights. To empower your people you must first make sure everyone has lots of information. Share everything. You cannot expect great results when people don't have a complete understanding of the business, so share the good, the bad and the ugly. Besides, withholding information creates mistrust, and no team can function effectively where there is an absence of trust.

Decide to not interfere with the process of getting things done. Allow people to make decisions and plan strategies for completing tasks. People will naturally rise to the level of responsibility you give them. Don't micromanage! Share your power by asking for input from your team. It is quite ok for the boss to say, "I was thinking of doing it this way. What do you think? Can you see any problems that may arise from this method? Do you know of a better way?" This is part of working with your team to uncover problems and provide solutions. Consider that you are in partnership with your team players/ employees.

Another important strategy for empowering your employees is to resist solving everyone's problems. Have them bring you three possible solutions and then ask them which one they think is best and why? If you agree, then give the go-ahead. If you don't, then present a case for your opinion and see if the employee can find flaws in your solution. Work together until you get it right. Odds are you will never have to re-evaluate a decision. Empowered employees usually make good decisions (because they are informed). If someone goofs up, try to learn from it and move on.

If you've never let your employees make decisions before, then you may be very reluctant to just let them loose and start directing the business. That's understandable. There are simple things that you can do to keep your finger on the pulse without manipulating the processes and outcomes.

First, you need to set up weekly one-on-one meetings with your employees. You will notice I give this instruction frequently in this book. That is because it is so important to your being able to successfully engage your people. These meetings should be scheduled in as a priority for each employee you manage. If you have too many direct reports to work with in this way, then decide who your key people are and make them team leaders. They can have scheduled one on ones with their crew. The purpose is to see where you can provide support for assigned tasks and what obstacles may be looming up ahead.

A useful one on one meeting should run for thirty to sixty minutes. Have your employee tell you about the key tasks he or she is working on and provide direction where needed. These sessions are not a de-panting. Your employee should leave your office feeling well equipped to take on tasks, not humiliated and inept.

During your meetings, your employee should be communicating problems to you from time to time. Do as instructed above and have her come up with three solutions for each problem. Ask her to pick which solution she thinks is best. If you agree, then set her free to address the problem. If you don't agree, then point out your concerns and have her continue to come up with a viable solution. If your ego is not getting in the way, she should be able to find a very satisfactory solution in no time.

True empowerment also means providing your people with guidelines or boundaries. If you are going to give people permission to make decisions about the business, then they need to know what the limits are. If your employees are uncertain about how much power they have, they will be hesitant to just take action, particularly in cases where previously, making independent decisions resulted in a tongue lashing. If you want to enable them to move the business forward, then you need to be very clear about this.

How much money can they spend on supplies they order for themselves? How much authority do they have to extend credit to a customer's account without your permission? What procedures can be amended to make things simpler? Who can be hired or fired without consulting you? These are just some examples of boundaries that you may need to define for your people. Talk to them and find out what they are uncomfortable with, and provide them with the opportunity to gain clarity regarding their roles and the confidence to proceed with decisions.

Another step toward empowering employees involves soliciting their opinions and advice regarding decisions you need to make: "This is the direction we want to go in. How do you think we should proceed in order to get there? Is there a better place to direct our energy?" Questions like those can be very valuable. Don't ever underestimate the insight of your people. They see the business from a different angle than you do. Their perspective is crucial to your success. Besides, when you solicit their advice and opinions, you are telling them that you value and respect their expertise. This not only ties them to the outcomes of the business, but it also instils confidence in their own ability to make prudent business decisions.

Creating a work environment that is conducive to employee engagement requires you to make sure your employees feel the work they do is important in fulfilling the company's purpose. In order to do that you must make sure that your employees don't just understand the mission, etc., but that they truly contribute to the realization of those goals. Soliciting their input allows that to happen.

Employees who have the equipment to do their jobs well will be both engaged and empowered. There is a lot to be said for being able to work in an environment that feels efficient. That means having an office that is not a junk space and having equipment that functions properly. If you've ever had to work in an office with continually malfunctioning equipment, or if your office space doubled as a storage closet, then you know how frustrating it can be.

It is human nature to want to do a good job. No one really goes to work trying to think of a thousand ways to screw up, unless they've got some serious problems. As a leader, you need to see to it that your employees have every opportunity to be the best they can be.

When we start a new job, we are typically pretty keen to be outstanding and we expect that we'll have a properly functioning computer, telephone and other resources at our disposal. If we don't have those resources, then we expect that someone should care enough to make sure we do have them ASAP. Not having them devalues your employees, frustrates them, slows down processes and compromises efficiency. Don't be cheap and lazy!

The brains around you are your most valuable resource. Use the expertise and experience of your employees to develop systems that are efficient and move the business forward. Toyota does this. They have developed an employee suggestion system and actually implement more than 99% of the suggestions they receive. Involving their employees in their continual quest for improvement has paid off big time. Now manufacturers everywhere are aspiring to be like them.

I honestly have no way of knowing what the level of employee engagement is at Toyota, but in studying their philosophy and the culture they have worked so hard to create, I would imagine the level of employee engagement is quite high. Toyota is known for the value they place on their employees and their customers. Living that value has allowed them to be in a rather enviable position. There is a strong correlation between employee engagement and customer satisfaction, and it certainly makes sense that there would be.

In developing and refining systems for your company consider adopting a philosophy of continuous improvement and implement suggestions made by employees. They are driving your systems however inefficient they are.

Unless you provide a format that welcomes their suggestions for improvement, nothing will ever improve, and what worked ten years ago, may not work so well today.

How many things are done inefficiently in your business just because that's the way it has always been done? Employees talk to each other all the time and say things like, "Why are we doing it this way? Doesn't it make more sense to do that another way?" And the answer from the co-workers or even bosses will often be something like, "That's the way we do it," or "Agnes wants it that way. She says it's the best way." But "Agnes" has an ego problem and she is very short-sighted.

I have seen instances where companies have invited their employees to make suggestions, giving the impression that they actually valued the input provided by their employees, but then publicly shot down their ideas. These suggestions would surprisingly come from the most unlikely employees; the employees who kept to themselves, did their jobs and went home. They never tried to outshine anyone or be spectacular, they just did their work. They were the middle 54%, and shooting down their ideas caused them to become actively disengaged!

Even if the idea is not a good one, thanking someone for their contribution, telling them that you will consider their suggestion and privately soliciting their input in order to make improvements on the idea would be far less damaging to the company and would take the employee to a much higher level of engagement. That is what you should be striving for!

Chapter 4

"No person will make a great business who wants to do it all himself or get all the credit."
– Andrew Carnegie

Since I've been talking about empowerment, I should also spend some time on the fine art of delegation. You can't empower people to do things if you don't delegate effectively, or if you are convinced that no one can do a job as well as you.

If you find yourself working until all hours of the night long after your employees have gone home, then you are not delegating enough. If you find yourself delegating tasks that do not get completed correctly or on time, then you are not setting clear expectations and you are not delegating effectively. If you find yourself constantly checking up on your employees after you have delegated a task, because you are worried about the outcome, then you are a micro manager and a control freak. Lighten up!

Being able to delegate well is really important to your business and is an essential element in securing employee engagement. As a leader it will help you secure opportunities for promotion and business growth whereas trying to do it all will not.

Delegate the things that do not make the most of your talents or your time. Do the things you do best, and let others do the things they do best. There are numerous tools available to you such as personality profiles and aptitude tests to help you determine where people's strengths are. It may help you to have your employees take some of these, so you can figure out where their strengths and interests lie.

Another way of determining which tasks can be delegated is to have a look at your do list and decide which tasks are not confidential in nature, do not require skills that are unique to your position, do not involve strategic planning, and are not something your own manager asked you, specifically, to complete.

Tasks that can be assigned to your team players are things which are within the realm of capability/expertise of your people. These tasks can be challenging and different from their usual work, but only if you provide clear direction.

Delegating tasks will help your company long after you are gone, or if you should become ill for an extended period of time. Great leaders want their people to be able to get along well without them. If you are delegating effectively, you and your people will be stretching and growing thereby creating a stronger company.

When delegating tasks, it is important that you define them clearly. There should be absolutely no doubt about what you want done. If you are not sure what the desired outcome is, then you cannot delegate it. Please make sure the task is genuinely suitable for delegation.

My friend, Melissa had a boss who continually left everyone wondering what she wanted from them. She would send out an email asking for a particular thing to be done, but would provide few details. After scratching their heads for a while and conferring with each other, the employees would attempt the task. Of course, they'd bring their boss what they thought she wanted, and it would have to be redone. This would go on several times before her people finally got it right. The result was, they would continually miss important deadlines and everyone would get flack for it.

Perhaps the manager didn't fully understand what needed to be accomplished, or maybe she was just a terrible communicator. Either way, not communicating and delegating effectively cost the company valuable time and money.

Choose the right person for the job. Assess who on your team would be most capable of handling the job. If you need to show the person how to do something first, then do so. If the job doesn't need to be done exactly your way, then let the person find the way that works best for them. Tell them how you do it and leave the door open for them to improve on your process.

Understand that you cannot delegate a task to people who do not have the skills to do the job. You may need to train people before you begin delegating or delegate small segments of the job at a time. If you don't have the patience or the time to show people how to do something that is important in the completion of the task then find someone who does.

It is human nature to want to understand why something is important. No one wants to be asked to do something for the heck of it. Let your employee know why a task needs to be done and they will be more likely to do it in good spirit. They may also be able to figure out a more effective way to reach the end result.

Clearly explain what the desired results should be. Tell them how the task will be measured so they will know if they are successfully meeting your expectations.

Discuss the resources required to complete the task. You must agree with your employee on what they will need, or who they will need to meet with or get help from in order to get the job done.

Agree on a deadline for the job. Your deadline may not be realistic in the eyes of your employee, so make sure you are not going to get any surprises.

Provide ongoing support in one on ones and be available in between times to help out. You will have to do less of this as your employees master these tasks.

Be sure to establish a reward system for completed tasks and offer plenty of verbal recognition.

If you are delegating well, you will find the team is completing tasks to your satisfaction, and that morale is high. They will feel involved and excited about what they are achieving. If this is not the case, then you need to get feedback from your employees to understand where you are faltering.

When delegating tasks make sure your goals are SMART (Specific, Measurable, Attainable, Relevant and Timed). I discuss this in detail in Chapter 8.

As you begin the process of delegation, understand that there are several levels of authority that you will be giving your people. Have confidence in their ability and build their confidence by doing things gradually.

Initially, if you are not sure about how well a task can be handles, you may not want to give any decision making authority at all to the employee. For example, if you need the employee to record sales and balance the cash, you may entrust the person with this task, as it is usually something that is done in a particular way and doesn't involve decision making.

Ideally, you want to work up to allowing your employees to set their own performance standards and goals, and to be able to make decisions with minimal guidance from you. You don't want to be a parent to your employees. If you are clear about the desired outcome, and provide the tools and training to get the job done, then you shouldn't have to babysit or worry about their work.

Chapter 5

"I hire people brighter than me and then get out of their way."
– Lee Iacocca

All companies experience turnover to some degree. Many companies refresh their pool of employees by restructuring their organization every three to four years, and even though the change is sometimes good, it is always costly. Other companies just can't seem to hold onto people. Sometimes this is a casualty of the industry, such as in Hospitality or Retail. Those industries do tend to lose people more frequently. Nevertheless, if you own or manage a company where high turnover is an issue, you are needlessly losing a tremendous amount of money. Calculations for turnover costs can vary depending on the position, but typically they range from 1.5 to 2.5 times the annual salary.

When determining the true cost of turnover to your company, don't just consider hard costs such as severance pay, litigation, training costs, advertising and recruiting costs. The heavier expenses actually lie in the things that are not immediately apparent. For example, a restructuring can have a terrible impact on employee morale. Fear and uncertainty tend to de-motivate and distract employees, thereby lowering productivity. Being short staffed also lowers productivity, and stresses the remaining team members, which could lead to increases in absenteeism and the dreaded "stress leave".

The fall-out from turnover gets even worse when you calculate the customers you lose due to lost relationships with departed employees. Quite often the reason you have your customers in the first place is because they like the people they are dealing with. When you lose an employee, you may lose his customers too. You may also lose customers because the lack of staff has compromised the quality of customer service in your business. Botched orders, slow delivery, lack of stock, missed deadlines, and trying to recover from errors, all cost money.

Knowledge loss and knowledge acquisition have a cost as well. When someone leaves your company he takes company secrets, client information, technical skills and more with him. What's more, it will take his replacement an average of 14 months to get over the learning curve. That's 14 months of lower productivity, confused and perhaps frustrated customers, frustrated co-workers, mistakes in processes and any number of other workplace mishaps. Once again, it's money out the company window.

Engaged employees don't quit and they definitely don't need to be fired. Companies who successfully engage their employees have stellar employee development programs that encompass both soft skills and technical training.

Many companies limit their training initiatives to technical training, but that's a big mistake. The "soft stuff" is pretty hard for a lot of people, and considering most people's point of reference (ego dominated leaders, companies with a low level of employee engagement) it is ridiculous to expect people to be top performers just because you hired them.

Most leaders don't know how to engage employees from the beginning. If they did, I wouldn't need to write this book and businesses would never have issues with low productivity and efficiency. They also have difficulty recognizing the unique value each employee holds for the company.

If you feel like you are swimming in a sea of bottom feeders, then you either need to reassess your hiring strategies or reconsider your own efficiency as a supportive leader. This chapter will deal with hiring and developing your team.

Employers are often concerned about attracting and retaining good people, and so they should be. Everyone wants to have the best people on board. The problem is many companies are better at hiring than retaining, and that indicates an employee engagement problem. You can have all the sophisticated hiring tools in the world, and a screening process that is quite lengthy and involved, but still have difficulty keeping your employees. The problem is the company's leadership.

When looking to hire people, hire for attitude first. You can teach a lot of different skills, but you cannot teach nice, pleasant, happy or helpful. If your job candidate has adequate technical skills but incredible people skills, hire her. If she has outstanding technical skills and miles of experience but seems a little aggressive, then take a pass. You know what they say: people get hired for their technical skills and fired for their people skills. Save yourself some grief and put nice people on the shortlist.

As you examine your immediate hiring needs, think of your future needs as well. Great leaders hire great replacements. Make sure you are looking for people who will be able to fulfill your future leadership needs as well as your present support staff needs. It's good to have a pool of potential leaders in place so that you can offer better opportunities to your existing employees and shorten the learning curve for someone who has been given a new position.

When hiring, don't make false promises and don't hire people who have ambitions that your company cannot accommodate. If someone has dreams of running the company and you have a family owned business, for example, then don't waste your energy on that person. If he or she takes the job, they will become frustrated and quit because of lack of opportunity. Remember, frustrated employees are not highly productive. They are disengaged! A great team is comprised of people who find their work challenging and meaningful. Make sure you always provide as much variety as possible and that your employees understand how meaningful their contribution is to the company.

Once you decide who you are going to hire, be sure to pay them well. If you pay people poorly, then you will be forced to hire people who are desperate and likely still looking for a better job. If you hire good people and pay them well, they will be a lot keener to do their best for you and show their value. They will also be committed from the beginning.

Consider Talent: Don't look at what people can do, but rather what they can do well. Employees who are using their talents at work are going to be a lot happier than employees who are forced to do things that are not their forte; and you will be a lot happier with the results they create. Engaged employees are employees who are working in areas that maximize their strengths. They are excellent at what they do and derive great pleasure from being able to use their talents to achieve successful outcomes at work.

Understanding the difference between talent and skill set will be crucial to your being able to successfully assemble the right team. Here's what you need to know: after working on something you have a talent for, you will feel energized and excited about what you have accomplished. I get that feeling every time I write something I am going to publish and every time I deliver a training session. These skills are among are my talents.

Conversely, I know how to file my tax returns for my business, and I can get the job done correctly, but I dread details and I hate doing the job. Not because I don't want to pay, but because numbers and details make my head spin. After completing my forms, I am filled with a sense of relief rather than a sense of accomplishment and I am mentally exhausted. Even though I know there are many ways I can keep myself organized to make the job easier, I never make the time to do any of them and I begin to dread the next filing session. Clearly, I am not a talented mathematician and I would make a horrible accountant. In fact, I would hate every day of my life if I had to work with numbers and details for a living.

Be sure to ask people how they feel after completing a task. If they are energized, they are using their talents. If they are drained, they are using their skills. Unfortunately, many people do work in areas where they have developed skills but have no talent. Try to uncover your employees' true talents and find a way to place them in the right job. In order to do this, you must have well developed rapport and a strong degree of trust.

Assembling the right talent may mean that you will have to juggle people around a little, and you will likely have to fire those disengaged employees (and so you should), but taking the time to do this will pay off in the long run. When looking for employees, make sure you hire the best people possible.

Someone once commented to me that that is hard to do in some positions, because no one dreams of becoming a great CSR. I contend that hiring the right kind of people for the position makes it easier to show people how meaningful their work is to the company. Someone who enjoys the challenge of helping a customer solve a problem, or who feels a great sense of accomplishment when they turn an angry customer into a great supporter will always feel challenged by their role in Customer Service. If as a leader, you continue to support your people and show daily appreciation for their efforts, they will find their work to be meaningful as well. It's all about choosing the right people and doing the right things with them.

Of course, a very important "right thing to do" with your people is to train them. Zig Ziglar once said, "The only thing worse than training people and losing them, is not training them and keeping them." Needless to say, Mr. Ziglar is a man after my own heart. An untrained employee will quickly become a disengaged employee. A big part of supporting your people is providing ongoing training. By helping your employees become better, they gain mastery, increase confidence and self-esteem, and will automatically contribute to building the bottom line.

Once you get all the right people in place, understand that employee engagement has to be secured from a person's first day on the job. A warm welcome goes a long way when bringing in a new employee. So does having a system in place to integrate your new hires. It really doesn't matter what level the employee is. Everyone coming into your company should be put through a complete orientation process that involves the following:

A Welcome Reception: Now, I realize a lot of people will think this is a ridiculous waste of time, but do not dismiss this practice. It is common to have a send off party when an employee plans to leave the company, so why not welcome a new person into the fold instead of leaving them to feel awkward? Most people start jobs feeling like they are in everyone's way because no one will take the time to show them around and introduce them to their co-workers. Some *managers* don't even make themselves available when they hire someone new. They feel they are just too busy so they stick the newbie in a corner with an employee policy manual and tell them to read!

Zappos, the online retailer I mentioned previously, has developed a very interesting practice around hiring and securing employee engagement. First, they make sure everyone starts their job by clearly knowing what the company values are and they actually offer their trainees money to quit! They pay trainees $2000 to leave the training session if they think they won't want to work at Zappos. The result is that they save themselves a lot of money by creating commitment to the company and cohesion among employees. Everyone starts their job knowing what they are there for!

A Corporate Buddy: Giving your new employees someone to partner with allows your new hire to become better integrated onto the company. The buddy can provide a tour, introduce the new hire to co-workers, and be available to assist the new employee at any time.

Lunch and Learn: Having a best friend at work is really important in developing engaged employees. For the first couple of weeks, employees should take turns having lunch with the new employee. Leaders beware of the damage your bottom 17% (actively disengaged employees) can cause in this situation. When a new person comes on board, they spring into action trying to recruit your new hire over to the dark side. Make sure those naysayers have limited access to your new hires. Hopefully you will have fired them all and replaced them with good people.

Get To Work: As mentioned earlier, new hires are very eager to make a difference. Find out where their greatest strengths are and put them to work on something that is productive and meaningful right from day one. Do not have them do work that is not in their job description. For example, if you hire a Director, help him or her get into the job by assigning a meaningful project. They can partner with other people in the department to get things done and understand more about the business in the process. Do not have your new hire follow people around to "observe" or stick them in a room to clean up shelves. This is demeaning, unproductive and bad for morale. Each time you have your new hire do something meaningless, you drive him/her closer to the door. The unspoken word is, "we don't recognize your talents and have no use for them, anyway".

Deliver on Promises: A lot of companies get swept up in the excitement of hiring and promise things to employees, only to forget later. The new hire is left waiting for gold to fall from a bucket into their laps and it never comes to fruition. You may forget, but employees never forget. Be sure to make a list of the things you promised and set forth a fair timeline, along with appropriate objectives so you can deliver on those promises. Have a discussion with your new employee about his/her expectations as well as your own and provide support for continued success. By doing this, you will demonstrate that you have integrity and will move closer to building continued engagement and loyalty from your new hire.

Appraisals: New employees need lots of guidance and support in their roles, but they also need feedback from you. Be very careful not to fall into the trap of continuous criticism. As I pointed out earlier, criticism is never constructive, and is always destructive. No one needs that. Even the term "appraisal" sounds intimidating. Turn those appraisal sessions into a relaxed one-on-one mini-meeting where you can review goals, provide support and bond with your new hire. Remember, we all need to feel valuable, and disengagement is directly tied to feeling under-valued. Praise efforts, acknowledge accomplishments and look for the good. Never focus on the negative. Saying, "You could have done this better," is not conducive to the engagement process. Be friendly, not threatening. People are more inspired by warmth than coldness. An open, non-threatening communication style motivates and builds loyalty. That's what employee engagement is all about.

Continuing Development: How do you support your new hires in getting around the learning curve? Whether you have just hired from outside your organization, or promoted from within, everyone needs to have a plan for continuous learning that should include soft skills training. If you have hired someone into a management position, see to it that they receive ongoing leadership training that includes components built around developing skills in communication, leadership, team building, delegation, building trust, etc. If you hire a Customer Service Agent, give that person continuous relevant training as well. It doesn't matter what position the person holds in the company, they are deserving of the opportunity to cultivate their skills for their own benefit, and the benefit of the company. I have met many people who worked in companies and climbed the corporate ladder, but never took a course in anything that really mattered to the success of the company. Soft skills matter a lot and anything you do to tell your employees they are important to your business, will contribute to their level of engagement and put money in your company's pocket!

Strive to Create a Diverse Team: A homogeneous workplace team will not be as successful as a diverse team. Having different kinds of people from different backgrounds on your team will allow you to see many points of view. You do not know what you do not know. Be open-minded and allow yourself to benefit from other points of view.

When you think of creating a diverse team, think about hiring people from different cultures, age groups, genders, and even those with disabilities. There should be a place for everyone! Take the time to learn about different cultures and even different generations. We are working in a time when people from four different generations occupy positions in the workplace. Each has their own set of experiences and values that colour their attitudes about work and life in general. Add to that the diverse cultures that make up our metropolitan areas and you have a wonderful opportunity to gain insight into the changing needs of our society. Companies that understand this and hire people from all walks of life, do better than those who don't.

Create a Strategy for Continued Success: If you want your team to enjoy the kind of success that can thrive in spite of organizational or group changes, then you must employ strategies that will give your team stability. This means that as a leader you need to plan out what you will do if someone leaves the group. Even engaged employees can leave their jobs unexpectedly for reasons that even a great manager can neither prevent nor foresee such as if a spouse gets transferred, or a family member becomes seriously ill, or the employee suddenly dies. Always have a succession plan for each and every employee. You need to know exactly what you are going to do in an unexpected situation, so that you can keep up the momentum you have worked so hard to build.

Work with your team to document procedures. Anyone should be able to walk into a position and know exactly where to find directions if they get stuck. Not having a tried and true method of doing certain things, will turn every day business procedures and results into a crap shoot. Your team can provide you with a tremendous amount of helpful information regarding best practices. Develop and refine these together and keep everything documented. You don't want to lose all of your procedures when you lose an employee.

It is often said that the mark of great leadership is not how well things run during a leader's tenure, but rather how well things hold together after the leader has moved on. If the company or department falls apart after you have left, then you did not do your job well at all.

Chapter 6

"The world hates change, yet it is the only thing that has brought progress"
-Charles Kettering

Change is an integral part of the process of continuous improvement. It is necessary for growth to occur and so adapting to change must be a part of our everyday life at work. When perceived as a negative force, the news of upcoming change is poorly received, and conversely, when perceived as a positive force, change is embraced. It's all about managing delivery and perception.

I was chatting with an employee of a large pharmaceutical company that had delivered news to their employees that after one year they would be moving one of their offices to another city, thereby leaving a large number of employees without jobs. The company regularly conducts employee engagement surveys and typically receives good reviews from its employees. After compiling survey results from the different departments, it was discovered that the team with the highest level of employee engagement was the team that would soon be out of work! You would think that they would find it increasingly difficult to stay motivated at work and to even care about what happened to the company, but they didn't feel that way at all! They continued to adhere to the company values and worked with incredible dedication. They did not perceive that they were being used as pawns. Nor did they feel bitter about the business decision that was made that would leave them without employment. What does that say about the company they were working for? What do you think of the leadership ability of their managers? Not everyone could pull that off so successfully. Most people wouldn't even dream it was possible, but it is and it can be replicated in any company that cares to engage their people!

So how does a leader manage to keep the team enthusiastic in the face of drastic change? One way is to manage perceptions. If your team perceives that they have no control over the process or outcomes, then they will be more likely to resist. But how can you know what the perceptions will be? Usually the boss is the last person to know.

This is where your relationships with your employees are especially important. If you recall the Gallup Management Journal statistics, 29% of employees are engaged, 54% of employees are disengaged and 17% of employees are actively disengaged. Your top 29% are your allies. Use them to influence your middle 54%. You will never be able to influence the bottom 17%, so don't bother trying.

Many bosses spend a lot of time and energy trying to convert their actively disengaged employees. You should just let them go. They are poison to your organization and contribute nothing of value at all. They will always stand in the way of progress and will take others down with them. No matter how long they have been with your company, no matter how much they seem to know, realize that they will do you more harm than good and need to be dismissed.

The middle 54% can be influenced by either the top or the bottom. They sit on the fence, but would like to be inspired to be better. They would like to be given a challenge and be made to feel like valuable contributors. Identify who your top 29% are and who comprises your middle group and use the top to influence the mindset of the middle.

Speak of the benefits of the impending changes to your top group. Your top 29% will tell you what the climate is on the floor when you are about to make changes. They will also be able to tell you what objections will likely come up in a meeting that announces the changes. This is powerful information so meet with your engaged employees before the "big" meeting and use the information you get from your most engaged employees to prepare for the objections. People accept change more readily when they understand how it will benefit them, so when crafting answers to your objections, consider what benefits the changes will bring forth that will be good for both the company and the employees. Please have your top employees contribute to the development your presentation. This is very important.

Professional sales people always speak of the benefits of their product and they prepare for the objections the prospect may come up with. They practice both their pitch and their answers in advance of any sales call. They don't want to lose the opportunity to generate enthusiasm for their product and close the sale. Learn from sales people because we are all in sales!

Leaders have to sell their ideas all the time, and they need those basic sales skills to prepare people for change. They also need to be able to work with their people to find the best solution to a problem. That is what professional sales people do all the time.

Once you announce the changes, your engaged employees should spring into action and speak of how exciting the changes are. They should let people know how beneficial the changes will be to the business so that they can effectively generate enthusiasm. Remember, your engaged employees are already excited about their work and their role in progress of the company. They will naturally want to help you make the company better.

Ideally, we would want all employees to be a part of the decision making process that drives organizational change, but this is rarely possible. The result is that sometimes we have to implement changes that are driven from above. What's more, we may not even agree with the changes at first glance. If changes are made with the company vision in mind, as a leader, you can always refer to the vision and values of the company. Never tell your people, "I don't agree with the changes, but I didn't make the decision." That sends the wrong message. That says, "I don't expect cooperation from any of you. In fact, I'd be surprised if you went along with this at all, and I'd be ok with that." Where would the company go with that attitude? You can bet it wouldn't be far. In fact that's a major reason why companies fail to execute change.

As a leader in your company, it is your responsibility to praise the company and to give all of your support to its initiatives. In fact, you should demonstrate enormous passion for the work you do as a contributor to the business. If you consider your role to be important in helping the company achieve its goals, and you are enthusiastic about the direction you are heading, your enthusiasm will positively affect everyone around you. Your top 29% will be especially supportive, and you need them to be.

Once you begin to leverage the influence of your top 29%, you should see positive changes begin to unfold, but that's only part of what you need to do to create unity and loyalty. If your people trust your leadership, you will find implementing change to be much easier than if you are considered untrustworthy. The following are things you should reflect on when going through organizational change.

Announce Changes Early: Child rearing experts tell us when we want to put our children to bed we should let them know in advance that they will soon have to put on their pyjamas. If you spring the news on your children suddenly, you will be more likely to have to deal with a tantrum. That's human nature, not just the nature of children. People resist change less, if they have a little warning that they will soon be expected to do something else.

Information Sharing: How you present information to your employees and what you present is very important. Hold nothing back. Present the information in newsletters and meetings and address the concerns of your employees.

Make sure everyone knows what to expect. Letting imaginations run wild will harm the level of employee engagement.

Keep Things Positive: Avoid having your employees work under a sense of impending doom. Do everything you can to keep the atmosphere light and positive. Speak of the good that will come of the changes, not the hardship.

Mission, Vision and Values: Speak of the mission, vision and values of the company and how the changes relate to these. Live the values. Don't let anyone perceive you as being a hypocrite.

Integrity: Resist the temptation to do anything that may cause your integrity to be questioned. This is always important, but during change, your bottom 17% may try to find a way to make you look untrustworthy in the eyes of their co-workers. Don't give them any reason to think you could ever be sly or sleazy.

Support Your People: Be sure your employees have all the tools they need to cope. That means training, and counselling, if necessary. Not all companies have the resources to do that, but at the very least give your employees a couple of books to read to help them out. Choose your titles carefully and present them in a non-threatening, open manner. Don't be a dork and anonymously mail them to people on your firing list (I know a coward who actually did that).

Understanding: Understand that we all deal with change differently. Some people are natural worriers and may have a million concerns. Others will embrace the changes and see them as an opportunity. People will jump on board at different times and as leader, your job is to make the transition as smooth as possible.

Protect Your People: In so much as you are able, do what is right for your employees. They will trust you if they know you have their backs, and they will work with you, rather than against you. Stand up for them and negotiate the best outcomes for them, if need be.

EllisDon CEO, Geoff Smith asked in his company blog what the secret to leadership was. The secret is there is no secret. There is no single thing a person can do that will generate strong business results or inspire people to want to be better. Life is more complicated than that. Great leadership happens in the continual striving to be better at communicating with people and it involves committing to doing a number of things alongside your followers in order to achieve your vision.

Chapter 7

"Coming together is a beginning; keeping together is progress; working together is success"
- Henry Ford

The people you work with can make or break the way you feel about going to work every day. Talent aside, if you like your co-workers and have rapport with them, you will find it a lot easier to find pleasure in what you are doing. If everyone on the team is committed to doing their best and if you are fortunate enough to work in an environment that is free from pettiness and cut throat behaviours, then you are probably reasonably content with your employer. The moment negativity sets in is the moment things begin to fall apart. Your actively disengaged employees thrive in these treacherous environments. They love chaos and they give energy to those behaviours while they suck the life out of everyone around them.

The best thing to do with your actively disengaged employees is fire them. Pay them a severance and make them go away. Do not ever try to constructively dismiss them or try to make them miserable by being a bully. That will backfire on you and you will lose whatever loyalty your other employees have toward you and the company. The least aggressive thing would be to simply create an environment that is so positive and pleasant, that they begin to feel they don't fit in and quit. That could take a long time, though.

Having said that, a pleasant positive environment is exactly what you want to establish in order to build and secure employee engagement.

Celebrate: Don't wait for an excuse to inject a little life into your workplace. Bring in a cake or some doughnuts to your staff and tell them you want to thank them for all that they do. You can be sure that if you do this on a regular basis, they will begin to willingly do more. When I was a manager, I used to bring cake into my office every Friday. In spite of receiving criticism, I persisted, and it paid off. Any time I needed a favour, my staff were always willing to step up. Because I did what no one had done before, I was perceived as being kind and thoughtful. It is human nature to want to return kindness. Treat your employees with kindness and generosity and be thoughtful in every possible way. You will always be glad you did.

Another way to celebrate successes is to establish a fun routine. Sales people often ring a bell when they get a sale. It is a small action that says a lot. It is an honour and a privilege to be able to ring the bell. Use your imagination and as always, solicit input from your employees and see what they might come up with.

Socialize. Take the time to get up from your desk and ask people how they are and what's new and then listen for the answer! Ask people about their kids or pets and be sincerely interested. Ask them nicely about the projects they are working on and take the opportunity to answer the phone, or do the things you don't normally do. You can even have them show you how they do things. This is known as Management by Walking Around (MBWA). Nobody will care about you until you show you care about them. When your employees feel you genuinely care about them, they will give back ten-fold.

A friend once told me he suggested to his boss that he get out and talk to his team instead of spending his day in his office with the door closed. His boss, a department VP, told him he prefers to get to know people by working with them. He wasn't the type of person to just go talk to people. These are his employees, so you can imagine what happened to the productivity of the department. Employees became increasingly discontent, expectations became unclear, and they couldn't go ask their VP questions because he was unapproachable. As ambitious as he was (he was awarded Canada's Top 40 under 40), he had terrible social skills and was very poorly chosen for the role. Sadly, that is a common occurrence in many companies.

Another friend told me about her director who sits in his office listening to his Ipod with earphones in his ears. When you plug your ears up with something the message will always be, "I am not interested in talking to you". It's the same as closing the door to your office or telling people to get lost.

Give a compliment. Think of something nice that you can say about each and every employee, and then go tell them. Always be sincere and please keep it related to work. Use your head and do not comment on things that will get you charged with harassment! Telling someone you admire their persistence, or their attention to detail is a form of recognition and it shows appreciation (something we all want). Doing this regularly will gradually increase the level of engagement among your employees.

Did you know that when you tell people nice things about themselves, that they feel obligated to live up to your impression of them? You will get more of a good behaviour if you make a point of acknowledging it by stating your admiration for that quality. Dale Carnegie called that, "Giving people a fine reputation to live up to".

Support a cause: Work as a team to do something that is good for the world outside of work. Get your group together to raise money for a charity. Everyone should choose a cause together and decide what you will accomplish as a team in support of the cause. Whether you decide to have a golf tournament, a walkathon, work in a soup kitchen, or hold an office lottery, let the charity be something that brings all of you together. Have staff members contribute in some way to build excitement around what you are achieving for your chosen charity, and have fun with it! Many companies try to give back to the community they serve. If your company doesn't do enough, you should get busy!

Start a club: Team building is enhanced when work groups do things together that have nothing to do with work. Some office club ideas could be a book club, a wine club, drama club, sports/ fitness club, a speakers group, etc. Use your imagination. When workmates have fun together outside of work, they gain the opportunity to see their co-workers in a different light. Developing friendships with co-workers is important. Employees who feel isolated will not be engaged.

Schmooze: A little social time over lunch or after work can be fun, too. Whether you have a pot luck lunch or bring in some pizza, as the boss you need to give permission to people to enjoy their time together. No working lunch breaks, please.

Many employees feel obligated to stay late or eat at their desks and work through lunch. This is quite often because the boss unwittingly makes people feel they should. Make a point of telling people to use their breaks, and use your own while you are at it. The mental health of your employees is extremely important. Insisting that employees use their breaks and enjoy them will be far better for productivity in the long run. Be sure to model the behaviour you want your employees to use.

Similarly, don't call or email your employees during their time off or when they are sick. I often hear stories about bosses sending emails to their employees late in the night. The message you send is that you expect your employees to have no life beyond work. That is unfair and completely rude!

Be spontaneous: There is nothing more fun than having a pleasant surprise at work. Whether it is an impromptu baseball game against another department, or having your employees walk into a balloon filled office in the morning, spontaneity and fun will inject energy into the workplace and boost productivity!

Having a light hearted working environment doesn't mean your employees will goof off all day. What is does mean is that productivity rates will increase as stress decreases. The more strain placed on your employees; the more likely they will be to miss time. Employees who miss time put strain on their co-workers, causing a vicious cycle of negativity, disengagement, low productivity rates, lost customers, etc.

The good news is that you really don't have to spend a lot of money to build cohesion and boost morale at work. You really only need to spend the time thinking up some cool ideas, and you can do that in the car on the way to the office! Besides, if you've got a team, you got a wealth of creativity and energy at your disposal.

Chapter 8

"If you don't know where you are going, any road will take you there."
– Lewis Carroll (*Alice in Wonderland*)

I love having goals. I will never understand how some people can go through life with nothing to strive for and no desire to achieve anything. What I can understand, however, is how people can lose focus and stagnate. Organizations do it all the time and so do the people who work in them!

Previously, I wrote about the importance of keeping objectives clear for your employees. Objectives should relate to the mission, vision and values of the company, but they should also allow for the professional development of your team.

Performance reviews provide an opportunity for management to lay out performance expectations for each employee as well as to plan for the personal growth of each team member. Employees who receive a review every six months and who are given the opportunity to achieve more in the company through training, etc. will be more engaged than those who receive little or no feedback or training.

A friend of mine worked in a position for nine months and never received any goals from her director until a couple of weeks before the performance review! What a ridiculous way to work with your employees!

Not only should she have been given a set of goals to strive toward, but she should also have been consulted regularly regarding her progress toward those goals. Just because you give performance reviews once or twice a year, doesn't mean that you should never refer to the goals before then. There should be no surprises when review time comes. Managers should be reviewing the objectives monthly or at least on a quarterly basis. Coaching for performance should be a natural part of your relationship with your employees.

Key Performance Indicators: As a manager, you need to be able to quantify performance. This means identifying key performance indicators such as sales, turnover, order fill rates, receivables, etc. Once you know what those indicators are, you can decide which are most relevant to each employee and start measuring. You will need to have a system in place to allow for that beforehand. Set up your measurement systems and use them to help your employees develop goals around them.

Give all of your employees some goals to work on six months prior to any performance review. A common acronym used in goal setting is SMART. I will explain it here so you can begin setting goals with your people.

Specific: Your employees need to know exactly what you are expecting from them. Goals should be very specific because if they are too broad, they will not likely be reached. For example, having a goal to increase employee engagement is not as specific as saying what you will do to increase employee engagement.

Measurable: You need to know how much you want to increase or decrease something by, so use your key performance indicators to give you something to measure. For example, it is better to say that you are going to increase production by 20% than to simply say that you are planning to increase production.

Attainable: Don't make your goals out of reach. It is unfair to set your employees up for failure. You may want to increase sales by 90%, but if that is not realistic, it will only discourage your employee.

Relevant: Goals need to be relevant. That's a no brainer, really. If the goals fail to make sense, or have no significance to your employee, they will be discarded. Your employees should be setting their own goals for this reason. Your job as a leader is to facilitate the process.

Timed: Deadlines motivate people. Set goals that have timelines that are both long term and short term. Your short term goals can be part of your weekly one-on-one meetings. Long term goals can be set for six months if you are doing appraisals every six months as you should be.

Personal: All goals should be personal as they are about the achiever. Don't talk about what the department is going to do in a performance review. Talk about the individual's contribution to what the department is going to do.

Post: Have your employees place their goals where they can see them. If they end up in a drawer, they will be forgotten. I use the calendar in my email program and sticky notes to help me remember my goals. Whenever I have a brain dead moment during the day, I glance at my note and find what I should be working on for the week. The calendar holds my long term goals and reminds me of what I should be gearing up for. It helps me stay focused. I find if I don't do that, then anything is bound to distract me.

Positive: Goals should be expressed positively since positive energy stays with us longer than negative energy. Rather than saying you want to decrease turnover, say you want to increase employee retention.

I once saw a cartoon of a guy leaving his boss' office with a shoe stuck in his behind. The caption stated that he had just received his performance review. Unfortunately, that is what most people experience in a performance review. They get to hear about all the mistakes they made and leave feeling like they've been kicked around a few times.

Performance evaluations are a necessary part of the continuous improvement process. They are a way of recognizing opportunities to improve, and should never be used to humiliate or downplay the successes of your employees. The focus should always be on achievements, not shortcomings. Someone once told me of a manager who gave everyone in the department a terrible review. The result was that no one was motivated to achieve anything. What the manager failed to realize was that their "poor" performance had everything to do with her inability to lead her team. What's really sad about this story is that the manager actually got promoted. I can assure you that whatever results she was able to create through negative feedback or fear are far less than what she would have been able to create through positive feedback and encouragement.

I regularly play a training game with my clients, which demonstrates the power of positive feedback. I divide the workshop participants into three groups and assign three leaders. The object of the game is to toss a penny against the wall and have it land on a strip of masking tape placed about two feet from the wall. The leader of each team is given a separate set of instructions which must be kept secret. One leader is to give only positive feedback to their team mates, and should continually offer encouragement by saying things like. "Good try." "Nice technique", etc. The second team leader is to say nothing at all. He must allow the players to just toss away pennies and make no comments of any kind. The third leader is instructed to give only negative feedback. He must make comments like, "That's terrible!" "What are you doing?" "You suck," etc.

I have to say that every time I play this game, the results are always the same. The team who gets positive feedback always manages to get the most pennies on the tape. The team who gets no feedback does much worse, and the team that receives only negative feedback gets the worst score of all. Interestingly, that team tries really hard to win. They support each other and offer encouragement to each other. They shut out the team leader completely, physically blocking his view of their performance. They do this every single time! It's fascinating, and people do this at work all the time. Think about your experiences with negative managers. How did you and your co-workers cope? Did you all gang up and complain about him/her whenever you had the chance? Were there things you tried to keep your boss from seeing?

Every performance evaluation necessarily involves giving and receiving feedback. Yes, you read correctly; receiving feedback. If you are to develop trust with your employees, you also have to allow them to tell you where you need to improve. No one is perfect, so expect that you may not always like what you hear. Be objective, don't make excuses and use the experience to grow. Check your ego at the door, please.

When you provide feedback to your employees, make sure you are able to quantify your judgments. If you can't back up what you are saying with numbers, then what you say really won't mean much. This is particularly true if you are trying to tell someone you are not pleased with their performance. You won't get through to anyone by speaking in vague terms and if you ever have to terminate that person due to poor performance, then you will not have any empirical data to demonstrate cause. Without that, you could get sued.

Employees should have the opportunity to submit a rebuttal of your review, as well. If they don't feel all of their accomplishments have been acknowledged, or if they feel there has been a mistake with your math, then they need to be given the chance to state their point of view and present the evidence.

Chapter 9

"The challenge of leadership is to be strong, but not rude; be kind, but not weak; be bold, but not bully; be thoughtful, but not lazy; be humble, but not timid; be proud, but not arrogant; have humor, but without folly."
- Jim Rhone

According to Bully Online, the web site of the UK National Workplace Bullying Advice Line, 66% of managers are bullies. That sheds a little more light on the source of employee disengagement, doesn't it? It's hard to be fully engaged at work if your boss is hateful and manipulative. Bullies have a way of making their targets feel completely inept at work. They are great manipulators, and that is usually how they end up getting promoted.

People only change their behaviour when they realize their behaviour has brought them an unbearable level of pain. If you are a bully without pain, you will never change. If you are a bully with pain, you may change, but when your back is up against the wall, you will likely revert to your old behaviours. People are who they are at their core.

What is the psyche of a bully? The bully at his or her core is a coward. Bullies are fearful and suffer from an extreme lack of confidence. They are egocentric, manipulative maniacs who get their energy from depleting the energy of those around them. The only difference between a corporate bully and a corporate psychopath is that the psychopath has not been wired with a conscience. A psychopath is incapable of change. The corporate bully can change if he or she wants to.

Corporate bullies can be either male or female and there are equal numbers of both. The females tend to be more covert than males, but they are equally destructive.

Several American states have been working on passing legislation that would ban bullying in the workplace and force employers to pay heavy compensation to victims. There is a realization that anti- harassment legislation needs to protect everyone, not just women, and racial or religious minorities. This is likely because according to studies, 40% of Americans claim to have been bullied at work.

Canadian courts are more recently taking a dim view of bosses who bully employees, particularly when the employee ends up becoming sick, taking stress leave or starts taking anti-depressants to cope with the pressure of the continual harassment. There is an emerging trend where judges forced the employer to compensate the employee as much as $1million. Subway, Honda Canada and Xerox are just a few companies known to have received such judgements.

In 2004, the Quebec government brought in legislation to protect employees from being victims of psychological harassment at work. Their definition of psychological harassment is, "any vexatious behaviour in the form of repeated and hostile or unwanted conduct, verbal comments, actions or gestures, that affects an employee's dignity or psychological or physical integrity, and that results in a harmful work environment for the employee."

That means that yelling at your employees, swearing or name calling, threatening to fire them or harm them in any way, could get you into very hot water. Anything you do to shatter the self confidence of your employees could be considered harassment. Please do not do any of the following:

- Berate employees either in front of others or in private.

- Constantly criticize or complain about an employee.

- Undermine an employee's value by demoting them or, taking away responsibility or authority they had previously enjoyed.

- Intentionally exclude an employee from meetings where his or her input would normally be important.

- Refuse to acknowledge an employee's contributions

- Overload an employee with an unreasonable amount of work.

- Set outrageous goals so as to set them up for failure.

- Refuse to allow your employee to receive necessary training, or cancel training mid stream because you decide it is no longer relevant.

- Do anything to intentionally frustrate your employee to the degree where he or she would be provoked to either behave inappropriately or quit.

- Force an employee to quit through constructive dismissal, or any other means.

I realize that some of these above items you may do inadvertently (not that that would be acceptable). It is doing these things in a constant manner and singling out a particular employee that presents the biggest danger to your company. The more of these behaviours you keep in your repertoire, the more likely you will be perceived as being a bully, and the more likely you will be to get sued.

If you have a bully working in your company and you are in a position to fire that person, you should. The bully is bad for morale and puts the company at risk on many levels. Any success they have in driving results will not be long term and you will lose money in less visible places (e.g. turnover, stress leave, lost customers, law suits, etc.).

If you recognize yourself as a bully, then you should get yourself a good psychotherapist. It is most likely that all of your relationships are toxic and they will continue to be until you decide it is worth it for you to be a better person.

Chapter 10

"I have never experienced another human being. I have experienced my impressions of them."
- Robert Anton Wilson

It may seem shallow, but we all judge books by their covers and we all create impressions of people based on what we see. When people look at your appearance, they pass judgement about your income level, your education, your morality, your social status, your degree of sophistication, how successful you are and your trustworthiness.

How your employees perceive you will affect the degree to which they can take you seriously and that will affect the results you get from them. If you come to work looking like you picked your clothes out of a pile at the bottom of your closet, that screams incompetence, and no one wants to follow someone who is incompetent.

It seems ridiculous that I should even feel compelled to discuss appearance in this book, but having been around a little, I know what's out there, and so I must speak.

Anyone who has had to hire people can tell you about the number of candidates that come through the door dressed like they're going to a ball game or the grocery store. Managers sometimes think that because they are the boss, they can wear what they want, so they come to work with torn jeans, wrinkled shirts or stains on their clothes.

Never go to work looking unkempt or really out of style. It affects your credibility. A bad dye job or hair showing 3 inches of dark roots looks horrible. Not getting your hair cut, neglecting to shave or keep a neat beard says that you are a slob.

Men with long nails and ladies who don't wear any makeup to work create the wrong impression. Take the time to look after your appearance.

Your employees will be much more receptive to whatever you have to say if you are not visually offensive.

I have seen bosses who regularly came to work smelling of booze from the night before. It's hard to respect someone who shows no self-control in their life and doesn't respect the work environment enough to come to work ready for the job at hand. Sorry, but no one is at their best when they are hung over.

If you don't look right for the job, then you won't be taken seriously, and you will have difficulty developing rapport with your employees and other co-workers.

Do you remember being a kid in school? Did you ever notice that the most popular teachers were the ones that looked the best? If they were physically attractive, they were automatically well-liked. If they wore really nice clothes, the kids all thought they were cool.

I had teachers who wore ridiculous looking things to school, and none of the kids wanted to have them for a teacher. They had a lot more trouble generating enthusiasm for their subject than the attractive teachers did.

Tips for Building Rapport and Generating Enthusiasm:

Set a high standard for yourself as a leader.

These standards should encompass the way you act and dress, the way you treat others and the expectations you have of yourself as well as of others. Give **yourself** a fine reputation to live up to.

Model the behaviours you would like to see in your employees.

If you want your employees to come to work on time, then you must do this as well. If you want them to treat others with respect, then you must do that as well. If you want your employees to enjoy work-life balance, then you must come and go at decent hours.

Give your employees the chance to shine.

Every time you allow an employee to shine, you raise your level of credibility and look like a really swell person. People like nice people and will take direction from people they trust. Make a big deal out of their contributions.

Recognize and praise all of your employees' achievements.

Don't let any good deed go unnoticed. Recognizing some achievements, but not others will cause uncertainty and breed mistrust. Since that affects rapport, you definitely don't want to be perceived as being unappreciative.

Do what you say you are going to do

Whenever you make a decision, act on it. If you say you are going to give someone a raise, don't renege on your promise. If you tell an employee they can have a day off, don't change your mind, no matter what. Never do anything to undermine the trust of your employees.

Walk around and talk to people.

Be a regular person and speak to your employees. Make sure you know everyone's name. The last thing you want as a leader is for people to feel you are too far above them. Leaders influence people from street level, not from the top of a tower.

Smile

A little smile goes a long way. A big smile goes on forever. Happy, friendly people are attractive to others. They are magnetic. Be as magnetic as you can. Happiness is a choice, not an accident. Choose to be happy and joyful and your joy will inspire those around you. Who wants to be in the company of a grouch?

Have a sense of humour

Don't take yourself or your work too seriously. Laughter opens the heart and eases the soul. Tell a funny story or a clean joke on occasion. When things aren't going so well, look for a little comic relief or try to find the humour in your situation. Dig around; you'll find it.

Ask people for their opinions

Everyone has an opinion. That I know for sure. Encourage your staff to express themselves and show their expertise. Your employees will feel they are important to you, every time you do.

Thank everyone for their contributions

Every day is a good day to say thank you. Say it sincerely and say it often.

Listen to what your employees are saying

When your employees take the time to talk to you, take the time to listen without distraction. No cell phones or messaging on your Blackberry. Repeat back what you heard to make sure you got it right, and validate concerns when appropriate. Ask questions, too.

Show your enthusiasm for your business

Enthusiasm is contagious. When you are enthusiastic, your employees will be as well. Positive energy makes you stronger and negative energy weakens you. Keep things light and positive. No doom and gloom. Telling everyone, "Sales are really down this year. I don't know how long we can stay in business like this," will not help you. Instead try, "Sales are down for now, so I think we all need to brain storm and see if there are opportunities we are somehow missing. We've got a great product and terrific people so we should be able to get past the dip."

Creating the right impression in the minds of your employees is important to your business. No one should be afraid of you. You will never be able to engage your employees if they don't like you or if they are afraid of you.

I have a colleague who claims he works for a raving lunatic. Every day he goes to work is pure pain. The CEO rants and raves and swears all day long. Apparently, he is a rather volatile egomaniac. I know if Bob worked for someone else he would be very dedicated and such a valuable team player. I am sure he is valuable even now, but perhaps only half as valuable as he would normally be. You simply can't get the best from people if you create the worst impression about yourself.

Afterword

Creating an environment that is conducive to employee engagement is not a quick process. Depending on the severity of your disengagement problem, it could take at least a year to get the results you want. It is important to understand that your dedication to creating an engaged culture will be well worth the effort. If you persist in doing all the right things, you can expect your bottom line results to at least triple.

If, however, you choose to remain complacent and work to maintain status quo, then you can expect your bottom line to be about 29% of what it could be. That's because if your company is like most, then only 29% of your employees are contributing to the bottom line that 71% of your employees are depleting!

Please consider performing the leadership development exercises that follow. They will help you generate the results you desire. If you have several people in leadership positions in your company, then consider the benefit of having everyone read and practice the suggestions in this book. Use this book as a selection in a company reading group or book club. The more people in your company who apply the information this book offers, the greater the impact it will have on your bottom line.

Leadership Development Exercises

Self-examination:

Examine the Ten Commandments of Leadership and the Seven Virtues of Leadership and note the areas where you fall short.

Ten Commandments of Leadership

1. You will guide, mentor and coach your people

2. You will set a fine example for integrity and professionalism

3. You will provide continuous positive feedback

4. You will take action

5. You will give clear direction

6. You will empower your people

7. You will accept responsibility for the shortcomings of your team

8. You will always make decisions

9. You will accept input from your team

10. You will establish trust

I have broken these commandments (list them):

Seven Virtues of Leadership

1. *Striving Toward Continuous Self-Improvement*

2. *Dedication*

3. *Sincerity*

4. *Generosity*

5. *Humility*

6. *Integrity*

7. *Wisdom*

I have lost these virtues:

What have these shortcomings cost you? Explain in detail.

What specific problems have you faced because of these? Write out your complete story.

What could you have done differently?

What can you start doing now to make positive changes?

Which changes are you committed to making right now?

Describe the actions you plan to take toward change?

Make your goals SMART (specific, measurable, attainable, relevant and timed). Make them personal and post them where you can see them.

Team Building:

Conduct these exercises to help build cohesion among your team members.

1. Gather your team together for a values session. Brainstorm a list of values that are important to your business and have your employees narrow the list down by voting on each value. Stop when you have come up with five core values.

2. Play a game called, "What I like about you". Randomly ask employees to take a turn saying what they like about a person on your team. Everyone has to say what they like about the person, but no one can repeat what someone else said about that person. Everyone should have the chance to hear what people like about them, and should also take a turn saying what they like about others. The boss participates in this as well.

3. In a group meeting, have each team member tell you what they feel their strengths are; that is, what they can do best for the team. Boss participation is 100%.

4. Have the group brainstorm ways they can use their talents to take the team to a higher level.

Building Rapport

1. Commit to learning something unusual about each of your employees. Assemble your team in a room and have them write something true about themselves that no one would imagine, and something false about themselves. Everyone should try to guess which story is true. Keep the stories clean.

2. Take turns inviting team members into important meetings with you. Work toward developing enough trust and empowerment to have them take your place in meetings.

3. Surprise everyone with a board game. Bring in your favourite board game and have the team participate. Depending on the number of employees you have, you can have several small groups playing at the same time and have winners play off against each other, or you can arrange teams that compete. They say you can learn a lot about a person by watching how they play a game. Who cheats? Who is a sore loser? Who accuses others of cheating? Who will be a gracious winner?

Recognition

1. Around 4:00pm every day, take the time to reflect on who you should give a special thank you to. Give praise to your employees every day. If they didn't complete something that day, praise them for working diligently. Don't say anything to

employees who did not work hard that day. Always be sincere.

2. Create a board of accomplishments and place it in the office where everyone can see it. Post in large print, anything that was accomplished by the team or an individual player. The board can be updated weekly.

Personal Effectiveness

1. Before you leave the office for the day write down all items on your do list for the next business day. Decide which of those items can be done by someone else on your team. Assign those tasks. Set time aside to meet with each person you will delegate the task to and go over the task. Set clear expectations for what exactly must be accomplished and when you need the work to be finished. Determine where you need to provide support, and then do so.

2. Set daily goals and use the SMART approach.

3. Take the time to just think. Having the time to think about your business will allow you to strategize better. Don't feel guilty for looking out the window. Your wheels are turning.

4. Take breaks and encourage your people to do the same.

5. Use your calendar/ daily diary to schedule in times for phone calls, meetings, specific tasks, breaks, etc.

6. Perform your most important tasks when you are at your peak. If you come to life in the afternoon, do them then. If you are a morning person, do them in the morning. Keep interruptions at a minimum during your peak time.

Employee Effectiveness

1. Encourage your employees to use the SMART goal system to assist them in meeting deadlines.

2. Have them use the same strategies as above to help them be more effective at work.

3. Meet with your employees to see where you can provide additional training in both soft skills and technical skills. Make sure you secure buy in from them before they start.

Personal and Professional Development:

1. Build a library of business books that will assist you in a variety of areas (strategic planning, negotiation, leadership, communication, etc).

2. Sign up for training. Join in on soft skills training with all of your employees be they front liners, managers and team leaders. You are not above them. You may appreciate the refresher and your employees will appreciate your humbleness. The sad truth about Leadership development is that the people who need it the most rarely participate in it. Those who do take the time to develop their skills, however, benefit greatly.

About the Author

Renée Cormier is the President/CEO and owner of POWERHOUSE CONFERENCES, a company dedicated to working diligently with businesses to increase efficiency, productivity and profit.

A specialist in the area of Employee Engagement, Renée has spent the last 12 years as a training and development professional. She has been an entrepreneur, worked for both large and small companies, managed both people and sales effectively, and developed systems and habits that brought her much success.

Renée uses her experience in Business and Adult Education to develop and implement training programs that show business leaders how to engage their workforce and get **guaranteed** bottom line results! Clients say her learning sessions are lively, engaging and valuable.

To ensure clients' business objectives are being met, POWERHOUSE CONFERENCES provides free employee engagement surveys to their clients. Once a learning plan is developed, an orientation is given to the client prior to the start of each in-house program.

POWERHOUSE CONFERENCES also provides follow-up coaching for the participants every 2 weeks for 12 weeks after the training to ensure smooth implementation of the learning objectives. Each workshop participant develops an action plan which is continually revised and is an integral part of the coaching process.

Passionate about the value of her learning programs, Renée partners with her clients to identify learning objectives that will increase productivity, efficiency and profit.

She also works with her clients to determine the areas most affected by the learning sessions in order to calculate ROI.

POWERHOUSE CONFERENCES provides clients with flexible scheduling and payment options to make it easy to achieve organizational effectiveness! We believe all businesses should be able to afford both the time and the money to build a stronger and more effective team.

To learn more about Renée Cormier and POWERHOUSE CONFERENCES, or to arrange a consultation, please phone (905) 593-2778 Email: renee@powerconferences.ca.

You can also visit her Website: www.powerconferences.ca. Or visit her blog: http://reneecormier.wordpress.com.

Renée Cormier originally hails from Sydney, Nova Scotia, and currently resides in Burlington, Ontario, with her husband Martin and their children. Engaged for Growth is her first published book.

Bibliography / Recommended Reading List

Buckingham, Marcus, and Curt Coffman, First, Break All the Rules, Simon & Schuster, 1999

Chandler, Steve, and Scott Richardson, 100 Ways To Motivate Others, Career Press, 2004

Robbins, Anthony, Awaken the Giant Within, Free Press, 1992

Tracy, Brian, Focal Point: A Proven System to Simplify Your Life, Double Your Productivity, and Achieve All Your Goals, American Management Association, 2001

Waitley, Denis, The Psychology of Winning, Berkley, 1986

Maxwell, John C., Leadership Gold, Thomas Nelson, 2008

Swidall, Clint, Engaged Leadership, John Wiley & Sons, 2007

Wilson, Jerry R.,151 Quick Ideas to Inspire Your Staff, Career Press, 2005

Lloyd, Ken, 151 Quick Ideas to Recognize and Reward Employees, Career Press, 2007

Godin, Seth, The Dip, Portfolio, 2007